INVENTIONS AND DISCOVERY

MADAM C. J. WALKER AND
NEW COSMETICS

by Katherine Krohn

illustrated by Richard Dominguez, Dave Hoover,
Bill Anderson, and Charles Barnett III

Consultant:
A'Lelia Bundles
Great-great-granddaughter of Madam C. J. Walker
Author, *On Her Own Ground: The Life and Times of
Madam C. J. Walker*

Capstone
press

Mankato, Minnesota

Graphic Library is published by Capstone Press,
1710 Roe Crest Drive, North Mankato, Minnesota 56003.
www.capstonepub.com

Library of Congress Cataloging-in-Publication Data
Krohn, Katherine E.
    Madam C. J. Walker and new cosmetics / by Katherine Krohn; illustrated by Richard
Dominguez . . . [et al.].
        p. cm.—(Graphic library. Inventions and discovery)
        Includes bibliographical references and index.
        ISBN-13: 978-0-7368-6485-5 (hardcover)
        ISBN-10: 0-7368-6485-7 (hardcover)
        ISBN-13: 978-0-7368-9647-4 (softcover pbk.)
        ISBN-10: 0-7368-9647-3 (softcover pbk.)
        1. Walker, C. J., Madam, 1867–1919—Juvenile literature. 2. African American women
executives—Biography—Juvenile literature. 3. Cosmetics industry—United States—History—
Juvenile literature. 4. Women millionaires—United States—Biography—Juvenile literature.
I. Dominguez, Richard. II. Title. III. Series.
HD9970.5.C672K76 2007
338.7'66855092—dc22   2006004080

Summary: In graphic novel format, tells the story of Madam C. J. Walker, who invented a line of
    African American hair products and cosmetics that helped her become the first self-made female
    millionaire of any race.

Designer
Alison Thiele

Colorist
Benjamin Hunzeker

Editor
Christine Peterson

Editor's note: Direct quotations from primary sources are indicated by a yellow background.

Direct quotations appear on the following pages:
Page 21, from Madam C. J. Walker's speech before the 1912 convention of the National Negro
    Business League, as recorded by the NNBL; page 23, from a 1913 speech by Madam C. J.
    Walker; as published in *On Her Own Ground: The Life and Times of Madam C. J. Walker,*
    by A'Lelia Bundles (New York: Scribner, 2001).

TABLE OF CONTENTS

CHAPTER 1
HARD TIMES 4

CHAPTER 2
FOLLOWING A DREAM 10

CHAPTER 3
SUCCESSFUL WOMAN 16

CHAPTER 4
LASTING LEGACY 24

MORE ABOUT MADAM C. J. WALKER 28
GLOSSARY 30
INTERNET SITES 30
READ MORE 31
BIBLIOGRAPHY 31
INDEX 32

In the early 1900s, Sarah noticed that her hair was starting to fall out.

Oh dear. I'm losing more of my hair every day.

Sarah, you just work too hard, that's all.

Like many people, Sarah lived in an apartment with no indoor plumbing. She couldn't bathe often. Harsh soaps dried her hair and scalp. Many people suffered from scalp diseases that caused sores, thinning hair, and baldness.

I heard about a lady on Market Street who helps with hair troubles.

I'd like to see her if she doesn't charge too much.

Sarah went to see a hairdresser named Annie Pope-Turnbo.

I make all my hair tonics myself.

I'm losing hair and my scalp is sore.

I think a scalp treatment will help.

How smart.

6

Annie hired Sarah to sell her products door-to-door and give scalp treatments. Sarah now made more money than she did washing clothes.

Do you think this treatment will help my hair?

Yes, I do, ma'am. My hair used to be in worse shape than yours.

The trick is to wash your hair often and use this shampoo.

And you're sure that will help?

Hair cannot grow unless the scalp is clean and healthy.

Sarah also found time to take classes at a night school in St. Louis. Sarah studied geography, reading, and bookkeeping.

I must improve my mind if I'm going to improve my life.

7

By 1905, Sarah was a successful sales agent for Pope-Turnbo. But she wanted more. That year, Sarah moved to Denver, Colorado, to be near family. There she worked in the kitchen of a boardinghouse.

I'm sure I can sell products to women at the boardinghouse. The extra money will help.

I hear you sell hair products.

That's right.

My hair is so dry. Nothing seems to help.

It's no wonder with all the salt in the water. But I have something that will help.

Yes, but this one really works.

Really? I've tried lots of different products.

When Sarah had all of the ingredients from her dream, she began to experiment in her kitchen.

This doesn't seem quite the right thickness. I'll add another cup of petrolatum.

A little more sulfur . . .

Ooohh that stinks. Needs more violet extract.

I've finally got the right formula, Charles. I think it's ready to sell.

You look wonderful, Sarah. Your hair grower really works.

In 1906, Sarah married Charles Joseph "C. J." Walker. She changed her name to Madam C. J. Walker.

11

Madam Walker made up her mind that she was going to sell her hair preparation. She named her product Wonderful Hair Grower.

I've made 6 pounds today. I'll see how fast this sells, and then make more.

Madam Walker began selling her product to women in her church and neighborhood.

Good morning, ma'am. May I demonstrate my Wonderful Hair Grower?

I don't have much money.

My formula is only 25 cents.

Word spread fast about Madam Walker's hair grower. Soon, she opened up a small salon in her home.

First, I'll massage your scalp. Then I'll rinse it with carbolic acid.

Acid? That will burn my scalp!

Don't you worry. It's very safe. It will help your scalp grow hair better.

MADAM C.J. WALKER'S WONDERFUL HAIR GROWER

Madam Walker liked to keep moving. In 1910, she opened the Madam C. J. Walker Manufacturing Company in Indianapolis, Indiana. No longer did Madam Walker have to make her products by hand at home.

With all of the workers and the city's large railway system, we'll be able to get orders out faster.

Now I can work on a new line of skin care products, Charles.

While Madam Walker continued to make hair and skin care products, a controversy was growing over their use. Some African Americans did not approve of using hot combs, flat irons, or products to straighten hair.

They are trying to make us look like white people, with long, straight hair.

There's nothing wrong with kinky, curly hair. That's what God gave us.

Surely you are not going to shut the door in my face. I feel that I am in a business that is a credit to the womanhood of our race.

They did not believe such a thing could be done, but I have proven beyond question of a doubt that I do grow hair.

Everybody told me that I was making a mistake by going into this business, but I know how to grow hair as well as I know how to grow cotton.

Madam's speech moved Booker T. Washington. She showed him her power and determination as a business leader. The next year, he invited Walker to speak at the NNBL convention.

NNBL

Madam Walker moved to New York City in 1916. She opened a new Lelia College and salon in the first floor of a house she bought in Harlem.

Women, what paves the way to business success?

Good grooming?

Absolutely. That and hard work.

I never thought I could run my own business, until I took Madam's course.

Did you know she used to be a washerwoman, just like us?

As her business increased, Madam Walker spoke to church and women's groups. She encouraged women to succeed in business. Madam Walker showed African American women that they could run their own businesses.

The girls and women of our race must not be afraid to take hold of business endeavors . . .

. . . and wring success out of a number of business opportunities that lie at their very doors.

I don't worry about having enough money to feed my children now that I sell Madam Walker's products.

Being a Walker agent changed my life. I thought I would clean people's houses forever.

Madam Walker also offered her hairdressing course by mail.

Madam Walker continued to create new products and expand her business. By 1918, Walker agents were selling 17 different hair and skin care products.

The first step in the Walker method is cleaning the scalp.

My customers can't get enough of Madam's Wonderful Hair Grower.

Mine too. I'm sold out.

At the height of her business, Madam Walker employed thousands of people, mostly African American women. Her business had grown from a tiny attic in Denver to a business with $250,000 in sales each year.

You have a lot to be proud of, Madam.

I had few opportunities early in life, Freeman. But I built a company that sells products across the country.

In 1918, Madam Walker built her dream home, Villa Lewaro, in New York. She invited her daughter and granddaughter to live with her there.

Grandmother, your new home is beautiful.

It is wonderful to be able to afford nice things for my family and myself.

I believe strongly in helping the women of our race.

Madam Walker also gave generously to many African American groups and causes.

Madam Walker's products helped many African American women improve the health of their hair. Her popular line of cosmetics made her the first self-made female millionaire of any race in the United States.

I say to every woman in this room, don't sit down and wait for the opportunities to come.

Get up and make them happen!

Madam C. J. Walker is remembered for her creativity and ambition as an inventor. She remains an inspiring, encouraging voice for African American women.

More about
Madam C. J. Walker

Madam C. J. Walker was born Sarah Breedlove in 1867, in Louisiana. Her parents, Owen and Minerva, were sharecroppers and former slaves. Walker was the first person in her family to be born free.

Madam Walker was orphaned at age 6, married at 14, and had her only child, Lelia, at 17. Madam Walker was a widow by age 20.

After she invented Wonderful Hair Grower, Madam Walker put together the packaging for her product. She bought tins from the American Can Company. A man from her church, who owned a printing press, printed labels for the tins.

Some people falsely believe that Madam Walker invented the hair straightening comb. However, she did use a wide-toothed steel comb, heated on a stove, with Glossine. This method made hair look longer and straighter.

Madam Walker created the Madam Walker Beauty Culturists Union. Each member paid yearly dues. The money helped employees in times of need.

Madam Walker died on May 25, 1919. Her last words were, "I want to live to help my race."

After her mother's death, Lelia ran the cosmetics company. Lelia died in 1931. The company remained in the Walker family until 1985 when the business was sold.

Today, Madam Walker's Indianapolis factory is a National Historic Landmark. The building houses the Madam Walker Theater Center, a center for African American art and culture. Madam Walker's mansion, Villa Lewaro, is also a National Historic Landmark. The home is a private residence.

In 1998, the United States Post Office released a postage stamp honoring Madam C. J. Walker.

GLOSSARY

agent (AY-juhnt)—someone who arranges or sells things for other people

demonstrate (DEM-uhn-strate)—to show other people how to do something or use something

scalp treatment (SKALP TREET-muhnt)—the process of applying products to the head to help heal sores

sulfur (SUHL-fur)—a yellow chemical sometimes used to treat skin diseases

tetter (TET-tur)—a skin disease, often of the scalp, that causes sores and itching

tonic (TON-ik)—a liquid sometimes used to heal skin diseases

INTERNET SITES

FactHound offers a safe, fun way to find Internet sites related to this book. All of the sites on FactHound have been researched by our staff.

Here's how:
1. Visit *www.facthound.com*
2. Choose your grade level.
3. Type in this book ID **0736864857** for age-appropriate sites. You may also browse subjects by clicking on letters, or by clicking on pictures and words.
4. Click on the **Fetch It** button.

FactHound will fetch the best sites for you!

READ MORE

Hall, Margaret. *Madam C. J. Walker.* Lives and Times. Chicago: Heinemann, 2003.

Hobkirk, Lori. *Madam C. J. Walker.* Journey to Freedom. Chanhassen, Minn.: Child's World, 2001.

McKissack, Patricia, and Fredrick McKissak. *Madam C. J. Walker: Self-Made Millionaire.* Great African Americans. Berkeley Heights, N.J.: Enslow, 2001.

Nichols, Catherine. *Madam C. J. Walker.* Scholastic News Nonfiction Readers. New York: Children's Press, 2005.

Sullivan, Otha Richard. *African American Women Scientists and Inventors.* Black Stars. New York: Wiley, 2002.

BIBLIOGRAPHY

Bundles, A'Lelia. *On Her Own Ground: The Life and Times of Madam C. J. Walker.* New York: Scribner, 2001.

Madam C. J. Walker Papers. Indiana Historical Society, Indianapolis, Ind. (http://www.indianahistory.org/library/manuscripts/collection_guides/m0399.html)

INDEX

Breedlove, Sarah. *See* Walker,
    Madam C. J.

Denver, Colorado, 8, 26

Indianapolis, Indiana, 18

Lelia College, 17, 22

Madam C. J. Walker
    Manufacturing Company,
    18, 29

National Negro Business
    League (NNBL), 20–21
New York, 22

Pittsburgh, 17
Pope-Turnbo, Annie, 6, 7, 8, 9

Ransom, Freeman B., 20, 26

scalp treatments, 6–7, 12,
    13, 17
St. Louis, Missouri, 4, 7

Walker, Charles Joseph
    "C. J." (husband), 11, 18
Walker, Lelia (daughter),
    4–5, 15, 16, 26, 28, 29
Walker, Madam C. J.
    birth of, 28
    death of, 29
    hair problems of, 6, 9
    name, 4, 11, 28
    products of, 11, 12, 13,
      14, 15, 17, 18, 19,
      25, 26, 28
    speeches of, 21, 23, 26,
      27
Walker agents
    salons of, 17, 24, 25
    training of, 17, 22, 25
Washington, Booker T.,
    20–21
Wonderful Hair Grower, 12,
    17, 19, 25, 28
    invention of, 10–11